E[illegible]

and

Unnecessary

"Erratic and Unnecessary"

Cover and photography by Kaylee Ortega

Dedication

To my Opa,

Who made me love books enough that I just had to write one.

And Kaylee,

Who is my inspiration for most things.

1

-He took a step and his feet fell through.-

He was the one who broke the ice,

But the flower was the one drowning.

Down

Down

Down

She woke up clinging to the ground.

But all around,

There was no sound.

The ice had cut a silver gown.

Tonight.

A night

Went

Down

Down

Down

She woke up in a metal case

And never dug her way up from that place.

2

Primary waves and earthquake zones,

The focus of her plan.

Once upon a princely file,

He met a man who wouldn't smile.

3

Alas I say

When too tired to play

And fall straight down a tree

I get up just fine,

And start to climb,

I'll get home at around three.

But reaching rocks,

My house is sold

I've been gone for quite a while.

Till through the door

Comes out one more,

I do not know this child.

They ignore my calls

And run on past

Into the street for fun

The years go by,

I don’t know why,

I cannot feel the sun.

4

I sit still- minding my file,

Watching everyone run half a mile.

Under the pain,

My main-hearted gain,

Was never not-sewing my style.

5

The buzzing sound

Of those around

Inside

Outside

The glass

And I

Perch above the evening plate

The light from the beam of getting late

Inside

Outside

Rubber hand

The blue flickers seem to have a plan.

The stinging eyes

Of red red joy

A bland paper stands

As the decoy.

Yellow strings across my heart

I watch them from my pole

As men in blue and guys of glue

Interrogate the goal.

Fleshy ground

The cement burns

I step from up my bar.

Then pulling loads,

The girls in clothes

Take me very far.

I'll know it's true

What I'm to do

When all

I feel

Is fed.

But I’m getting faint

Of that red paint

Inside

Outside

My head.

6

God, let me tear apart my hands

This hatred stuck in me

I'm sick of looking in the mirror

And not liking who I see

God, let me smash my face into the walls

And ruin what I know-

I'll never stop despising

No matter how fair I grow

God, let me rip out every hair

That sickens every strand

Of every fiber in my being

That tells me I am bland

God, let me scramble up my brains

Because my thoughts are never grand

I'm sick of analyzing myself

And not liking who I am.

7

"I know you don't believe me

In this letter I write to you

But my eyes have not deceived me

And I will always honor you

But I promise that I saw it

In this letter description be

The winged people on the ceiling

Of a chapel just for me

Their eyes should fall through the floorboards

But they like to stay in place

And so I write this letter to you

Though I know it will disgrace

But I promise that it happened

Even if you do not see

The winged people on the ceiling

Of a chapel just for me."

8

Don't chase them off the property

They owned

The land

Before

And there they died, and buried,

The friends that could

Do nothing

More.

9

The

Structure

Of a face

That's bringing

Bones

That crack

And needles singing

Wives

That create

Many faces

In the little

Tabled places

10

She's either always swinging

Along a line of fault

While volcanoes erupt

Just to open up the vault

And then a cage is freed

From nothing that she knows,

The core-mantle boundary

Had once been called a home.

A delta meets his end

As ozone comes to play

So she makes fun of the troposphere

And the contrails go away

In her free time, she sank ships

As the hurricanes are cops

Then down went all the stratus

And the cirrus stayed on top.

(I want to remember all my terms, those important things to know, and I say I hate forgetting so I gave them a place to go.)

11

Octagons act like cowards.

The penumbra,

The flower,

The circle,

The sun, the moon, her stars and sky.

And then she got tired.

12

My darkened friend around the corner

Touched the rope

I saw it float

But disappeared she did when say

Only today

She saw us play

Her teeth are sharp and no one sees

Her claws in size

How she kills mice

Tall as a house, she hides on by

My darkened friend hides in my mind

Only comes out

During the drought

My room is bland when she's away

The corners shake

And what we'll make

I guess she can come again today

And I pray that she will stay.

13

There once was someone angry

Whom never did I know

Who'd throw away their pennies

In a timeless way to go

Away

And slowly drain their life span

When nothing ever slept

Then meet up with the dying man

And torment the souls they kept.

14

Inside an old cupboard

Patched up with dead fur

Bear with me, a Bible

Has memory of her

The blue cat gets itchy

The pink one is shy

The rag-doll across the room

Is on the wrong side

A legion of followers

Locked inside a box

Named after a phrase

Only remembered on docks

An underground neighborhood

With rules by an elf

But he remembers it started

When he jumped off his shelf.

15

My walls have ears

That listen up

And I have fears

That brim my cup.

I'm caged all in

These own four walls

Whose voices feel

Like they have calls.

I'll sit on far

Away the room

And never try

To pass on by-

The door.

For I do find evermore

Me leaving gave a crystal sore;

They will all see

Waiting for me

My nervous walks,

Around the halls,

Of a four-walled room,

That never falls,

Away.

16

I saw her,

Orchids, orchids,

Blooming from every sound

But her tears, they-

Orchids, orchids,

For the things she never found.

She came here,

Orchids, orchids,

And there was nothing that wasn't new

But her fears, they-

Orchids, orchids,

For the things she never grew.

In the nighttime

Orchids, orchids,

Was when the children cut her free

But her mind, went-

Orchids, orchids,

She knew they would never let her be.

Running swiftly,

Orchids, orchids,

Her stems shriveled just to cry

But her eyes, went-

Orchids, orchids,

And there was no reason why.

Little creatures,

Orchids, orchids,

Counting to the number four

But her cries, they-

Orchids, orchids,

When she washed up on the shore

Opened window,

Orchids, orchids,

It was all that she could know

But her thoughts, they-

Orchids, orchids,

There was nowhere she could go.

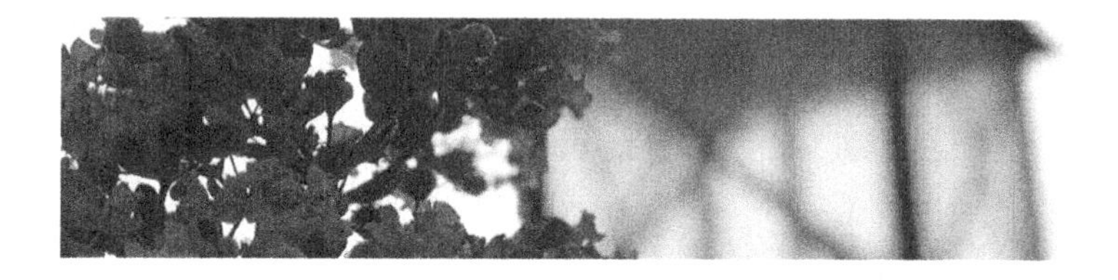

17

A friend that comes.

Within the night

A nifty

Fortified

Place above the ceiling

And the only thing you have to fight

Is your tall, unsteady height.

18

I lost my raptured smile

Three days ago

Half days ago

And all the paintings

I've entrusted

To sit peacefully amongst my walls

Are slowly

Very slowly

Ripping themselves off and becoming known.

19

Hickory dickory doo

The boy was sad and blue

And then he cried,

The boy had died,

And there was nothing to do.

Hickory dickory dar

The boy never went far

He never tried,

So then he died,

He never had anything to do.

Hickory dickory duh

The boy was only "the"

So then he cried,

And then he died,

Now, there was nothing he could do.

Hickory dickory doo

The boy had been sad and blue

But now he's dead,

He'll rest his head,

This is all that he can do.

20

Claw at the walls

But don't escape

Amaranth will await her fate

Just

Take

A while

Unfeeling stills

A little girl trapped under pills.

21

I once knew a man

Who never took any risks

He never laughed

He never fixed

He never made mistakes

So he never felt sad

But he could not be happy

If nothing went bad.

His family, all merry,

Did not visit his grave

(This dead man, so still now,

Had never been brave.)

They said to the keeper

When a letter they did receive;

"*He didn't spend his life living*

So what would we grieve?"

22

You’re stuck inside

The glass inside

And we will talk for now-

But I am tired

And I’ll be fired

If I don’t put you back somehow.

23

They know you're dying,

Addiction,

Of course.

And no one cares about your corpse,

Falling

Falling

Down the hill

Into the driver's seat and will.

-falling-

Anything that's falling,

(It will)

Of course.

24

I moved into a mountain

That covered up a town

Where nothing ever happened

And no one wore a crown.

I watched these people moving

As they went off on their day

Though nothing ever happened

I could never look away.

So in time my body rotted

As one who dies must do

But no one knew that I existed

So in that chair I stayed to brew.

And my eyes could never close

But they never felt the need

Because I still watched those people

Like I did when I could breathe.

And my soul became engraved

In the mindless tasks they did

And people started talking

About a man who hid

Inside the mountain close by

Who protected them from flame

And nothing ever happened

And no one ever came.

25

Twin sisters, both, I plainly tell

Work with me at my cart

And the carnival we follow shows

That it's starting in the heart,

So when at dawn the students rise

My poison comes to play

And my martyrs come out on their deck

And lead the cast away.

26

An oval shot

The whole wood-caught

In basic times of grey

And-

Seeing me,

The timeless spree

Of running past the day.

Chariot pulled

Upon the stars

We jumped across a moat

To-

See the fill

Of orders till

The cups of tea that float.

And buttoned down

His sea-filled mug

The order of the day

For-

Her waited Nile

Just passed a mile

Of green-grey surface play.

The walled-in foe

Would crouch down low

The painted wall to be

So-

Falling fast

The oval passed

And never came near me.

27

They hated lights and shiny things

But neither was to blame

For they never looked even a bit

Like they had color in their veins

28

The vines will spread

Despite his dread

The crystal clear cuts above the sky

Are always figuring out why

The children live to see past ten

The men all old are finding when

But sacrifices must be procured

Despite the fact that nothing's ensured

And he awaits the purple tile

Of monsters who will wait a while

Those who will live after his pass

Sing a song that will not last.

29

I'm a living, breathing something

Who's death I do not meet

But I'm turning into powder

Beneath the dead one's feet

And the sun will blare away some

And up the stairs I go

And I find that some dead people

Reap what others sow

But spells might be cast at some point

And light begins to hurt

And I hate that getting quicker

Puts a red-stain on my shirt

I did, yes, stop my breathing

But no one here can know

I'm dead, I'm dead and dying

And that's just how it goes.

30

A plethora of faeries,

The cello, obsolete.

Everyone loathes the cyanide,

Of a rubatosis beat.

Amaranthus has a clock,

That will never stop its tick.

The anathema-like cupboard

Says lullabies really quick.

31

She sees the bruises on her hands

And wonders why they took

So long to appear after the fear

Of what she did had shook-

Her awake just late enough

For the stars to fade,

And she sat very still as she realized

This was not just another day.

They make it all seem simple

But there never was a cure

For breaking people's faces

And molding it for sure.

They took her up in boxes

And made her wait in line

And through the nailed crosses

She knew she was not fine.

32

To scrutinize a monster

Make steadfast your belief,

Don't tolerate or overrun

The integrity of grief.

Unnecessary, unnamed,

The roommate to the left

Makes meticulous and guile

Places you should have checked.

Foolhardy and immoral

The cattail faces west

If disservice becomes similar

On a fishhook you'll find rest.

Her earrings are obscure,

Her chamois a nighttime bin,

To videotape whatever

On an irrelevant, broken whim.

33

-Scarecrow oh scarecrow

I never seemed to see

The fact that you are lonely,

With no company.

Your disfigured shape

Scared off all your peers,

So you sit alone

Crying scarecrow tears.

-Scarecrow oh scarecrow

With the corn half way done,

Never have you spoken

Not to anyone.

How could you try

When looking at you makes them scream

You do your job too well, oh my

But what else could you be?

-Scarecrow oh scarecrow

Your bounty is all grown,

You have protected it all year

Yet none of it do you own.

Then down the hill your body goes,

When famine comes to town

Only to be picked up from your foes,

And burnt straight to the ground.

34

A swirling, downward spiral

Amidst a hurricane

Has never felt like it must

Fight for all its rain.

35

The sirens scream their burning blare

The dead surround us

And I'm tired

Of chasing after

The winds outside my dome,

I see nothing there

And so I stare

As if that will change my home,

But-

"There's nothing to fear"

They want my mouth to shut

And the sirens scream their share.

36

My hair is down

I wear a frown

Or smile when in bloom.

I see the fear

All crystal clear

I read inside my tomb.

37

I'm very sorry

For the folly

That the old ones make

To you.

And I get scared

Of how I'll fare

If I speak

To you.

Yet I stand a while

To watch your trial

And end up leaving early.

You do not remember

The child sender

That's brain might always be

On empty.

38

A grotesque, dusting, broken beam

Is a child setting free

A great big brook of words to spill

Is a pot with words to fill

He says to him

A great-loud whim

"*Create within this mold of death*

An angel with forever breath."

39

A curtain falls inside the room

The glass around will fail.

And sparkling lights inside the loom

Will one day finally be unveiled.

We never told you how to hide

The sand that covered up

The face that was scarred with cyanide

Which you pour into our cup.

The bejeweled sword that spoke to you

Hangs right above your head

And swinging down from where you stand

Are the spirits you have led.

You destroyed lands because of fault

And murdered those you passed

And never gave it any thought

Of who or what might last.

So they never told you how to rule

The land from which you signed

We crawled into our metal holes

And made up our own minds.

40

This isn't me

This isn't me

This isn't me at all

I'm in this tiny body

But I know I'm ten feet tall.

My hair should be much shorter

And this isn't my own chest

My nails get too long as well

And I get too much rest.

This isn't me

This isn't me

This isn't me, I'm sure

My mind may have been wired shut

And speaking might not be the cure.

My limbs are just too weak

And my eyes simply do not work

Though company is mandatory

In the shadows I do lurk.

This isn't me

This isn't me

This isn't me, I know

And nothing solves the problem

No matter where I go.

I do not feel like I am here

My body is not mine

This complex marching pattern

In my body is a lie.

This isn't me

This isn't me

This isn't me you see

My soul is stuck inside a rotting corpse

And I cannot be set free.

I do not want to know I belong

To the medicine I take

But complaining does not help since I

Feel as though I'm fake.

41

Knock on bottles

So

And melted colors

So

And breccia crumbles

As things mumble

So

42

The shy man drew

For very few

His red-capped child

Only filed

Away his pictures

Touched the textures

Very slowly

Very coldly

43

There once was a man not so

Whose name was unknown to his foe.

He died, they say

On an uninteresting day

What a depressing way to go.

44

My box is small

I'm cramped, is all.

Open up

I'm here

I'm here

You weep, I see

You hated me.

The man I fear

Is at the door,

Across the floor

One

More

Step.

(He can take more)

Took all of mine.

He knows he can take them

Every time

My box is small

You cannot see

The way I try and set me free.

Preach about the fall

(He does what's best)

A lady walks away

In

A

Hydrangea

Dress.

Open up

I'm here

I'm here

The smell within starts to disappear.

The ground wells large

(Your voice is faint)

The cars ahead are becoming late.

My box is small

I'm here, I'm here

I hear the bones around me steer.

Rotting

Rotting

One

More

Step.

Its dark, it's closed, the mirror's full

Around myself, inside my hole.

A sack of plants

His voice is still

I'm waiting till-

Hydrangea

Hydrangea

Hydrangea.

45

Coffin made of timeless ore and cracking slumber,

Open

Open

Open

It's the easy way out.

The villain rises from her undead resting point,

It drapes over her shoulders well,

(But none of them could say that.)

All we need is *a book.*

46

It cracks and strains

Despite the rains

Awaited lists

For fighting fists

She never thinks after the pain

That she has to have more than disdain.

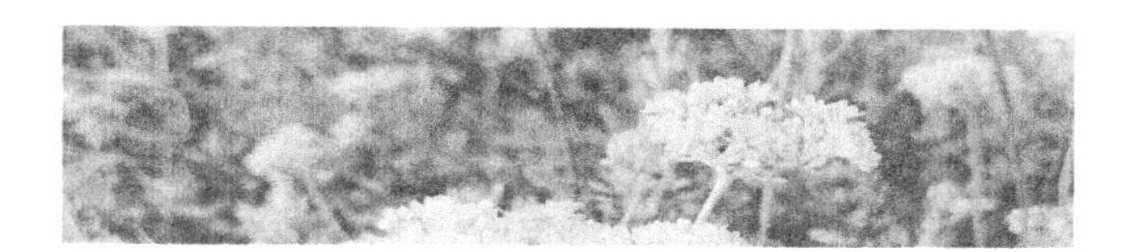

47

For sometimes

If it was quiet

And the night was

Late

Late

Late

If I didn't fight the sleeping

If I didn't fight the listening

If I listened very closely

And morning and midnight collided,

Mostly-

The full moon swaying dimly

I could hear it

And it may have been a crime.

48

On a shelf

(With button eyes)

A lovely chant;

Of her

(Demise)

49

A pinkish man

Without impish grin

Had child made of maze.

Winters hull,

A summer's blaze

And Father was away.

Patterned skin,

And dance within,

Her arms were stone and grass.

And down the hall,

A pictured call,

Could cart her lights and pass.

50

The stage is set for

Screaming

And I know I am not

Dreaming

For the clocks tick on their

Own

And I'm trying to get

Home

But all the doors I find

Are locked

And my nails are getting

Mocked

By the elders in the

Books

Who give me dirty

Looks.

51

I fear I'm going numb

And getting very boring

And I hate that I don't know

What lies underneath the flooring

Of-

My kingdom, and my desk

Gives splinters to the guard,

They'll come again so very sure

That it can't be very hard.

52

Lovely crystals cut way to deep

His death was soon and sudden.

He froze in his spot inside the cell

The monster around the corner swelled;

With pride, "*I'm sure.*"

With pain, '*I care.*"

The crystals came from everywhere.

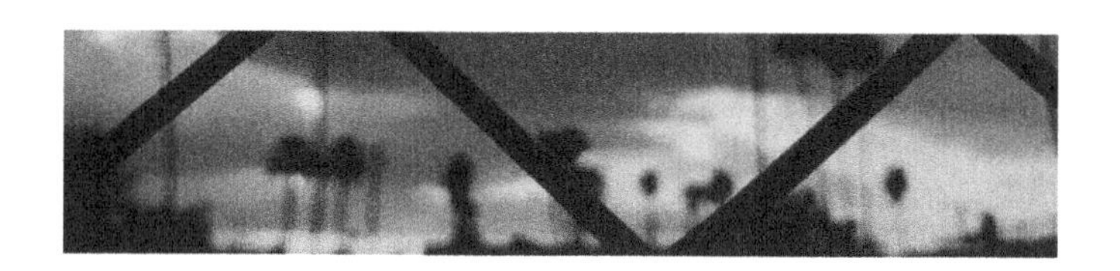

53

I'd like to live in a tree

Turn the plants to make a crown

The one outside my window works

Whenever I do frown.

If I could rent a treehouse

Just for a little bit of time

I could make my own small kingdom

Where everything would rhyme.

I would never get confused

Because every rule was mine,

The steps would always fit me

Because I made them all just fine.

My subjects would be the lizards

And every single bug

That couldn't live on the ground

Because they hated mud.

If leaves could be my hideout

For just part of the day

I think I could live longer

If you really want me to stay-

But I know that I would merge

Together with the bark

Because maybe I would finally feel

Like it was a work of art.

When every plant would die

My tree would stay alive

Cultivated off the something

That I know did not make me cry.

But trees are always with me

Little cities in the wood

If I could just rent a treehouse

I promise I'd be good.

54

This type of fire,

This type of sting.

Inside a cell with bells that ring.

55

Piano plays

Long songs to me-

And Mother stays away.

"If ever,

Here,

I need to go,

This song with you will stay."

But Mother hates to play these songs

Piano is a fiend.

When I walked back down the stairs

I'll tell you what I mean.

The coin upon his neck had crawled,

Told me to stop my climb.

And now I sit, my Mother used to knit,

But she plays piano just fine.

56

They come when I am lonely

And I don't get much help

And I find that voices really

Don't care about my health

So-

When sunshine comes as older

And I don't hide underneath.

I find their carcass colder

Than when I was glad to meet.

57

Red

Blue

Green

Loud static cars -

Crying.

Just like that;

I was done.

58

In the end

I'll eat the crows

That is how

My tale goes

59

I saw it as it made way

Under the ground and walls,

Even though I have no feelings

I watched her walk down all the halls.

For she angered all the people

And then started all the wars,

I recall the moments feeble

As they washed up on all the shores.

60

The danger lies within the snow

That soaks into her blood

And no one whispers of the foe

She left dying in the mud.

For never did they try to think

Such a tiny thing could kill

But as she walks on past their tents

They worried for her still

Because as they draw on near the pain

Of war within their midst

They know she will fight along her knights

Despite her many kicks.

How long can such a child go

Before they start to fall

When they realize who they're hurting here

Is ten times their might in tall?

What damage must a kid obtain

To get this far in war?

But the soldiers who all look at her

Cannot seem to find the core

She came to them amidst a storm

And that is how she'll leave

And painted in her pathways mourn

Are souls

That wish

To flee.

61

There's food on the table;

(A lovely display)

The food was bland,

He thought-

"I cant."

For

(Never)

Did he want to play,

Thinking

"Sleep is now the only way."

62

My family is of aches and pains

It goes on down the line

My grandpa has a headache

And my grandma has no spine

We do not know my mother's side

And flesh along his back

Goes

Crack!

But mother's leg

Is bruised and pegged

With needles on her mind.

My brother says his arm hurts

My sister lost her ear

My uncle broke his head ten years ago

And now he cannot hear.

And family and all those before,

Tossed on their side and coughed

And that, I say, leaves only me,

I do not break this curse

For my organs feel like boils

Had been stapled in me first.

63

A strong and yellow beam

From where the blue and white

Had once taken for cover

And the birds in which take flight

Are never ever breaking

As painted dots align

In clear, iridescent patches

That like to tell the time.

64

I found myself inside a shop

With bottles in a line

They were covered in old colors

That I knew would withstand time

For inside of them they held their past

And secrets of the lost

And I tried to ask the keeper

She had gotten them-but at what cost?

For they seemed to have no title

Yet they didn't look the same-

The orange bottle held some needles,

And the purple one held rain,

The green one rocked teeth asleep

That rotted over years,

And the one made of pure marble

Held a patch of dead man ears.

Inside of one I found quite large

(Hidden underneath some sheen)

I found a living heartbeat

That cried at what I've seen,

And the keeper told me something

As I made my way on out;

There would never be enough coins

To buy even one amount.

Because she had spent her whole life taking

Hunting fever, moving stars,

To find the right concoction

That would bring back her lightning scars,

And on her way, she made her friends,

And kept them to herself,

By coaxing them into sleeping

In the bottles on her shelf.

65

A yellow plate

Will swim too late

And search among us till.

Order still,

My worthy kill,

And bump the green-house gate.

66

I woke up with a fractured skull

And bags under my eyes

That packed up all my tinted shames

And labeled them with cries

They ripped open my mouth and stole

Away my pointed teeth

Leaving me defenseless

To the sharp pains underneath

My head still aches, now empty still

My nails all turning flat

And I never thought they'd ever know

That it had always been like that.

67

I caught a child planning

Hiding underneath a box

When I asked her what she was doing

Her reply got written on the clocks

Because her mother changed the loads

And her father broke the bearings

So her siblings ran around

While she was left despairing

And it got loud outside, to me

And she didn't disagree

So I took out a pen and pencil

And asked her "*What do you mean*?"

So she told me about hiding

And how easy it could get

She even wrote down a checklist

And told me with it, '*Never fret.*'

She said this was her own secret

Why she must still be alive

Was to get these words committed

Into every single mind

Because her mother told her quietly

As soon as she had started to live

That children are only valuable

If they have something to give.

She lost three brothers this way,

Those scary little things,

And she was absolutely terrified

Of what else uselessness would bring

So one night very lonely

As Mother changed a sheet,

This child crawled up on the writing desk

And wrote her story in red ink

Because a kid who writes down secrets

Cannot be considered dead

She told me that people wanted to know

How she had learned these things instead.

And her father came in suddenly

Breaking things as he went,

So she crawled a little further

Away as glass-shapes sent.

And she handed me some papers,

Said my own was meant to be

The title to her pension

Of a living memory.

So I took this book and kept it,

I showed it to the woods,

I let everyone I could find

Know exactly what they should.

And I had a special question

For when I read her fun,

When I get home all tired

What exactly have I done?

68

He walks down roads

Like he doesn't know he's walking.

So he has no

-Fear-

Of

Tripping

At all.

69

His eyes felt heavy

His mind felt dry

And with one final thought-

"I wish to die."

70

You're

Running

Running

Down the hall,

A tiny dog

With little paws.

A door that's closed-

You jump right through,

And falling

yet

You start anew.

71

I know myself better than you

Can you read my own mind?

I don't suppose a telepath

Would get around just fine.

But my brain has become all my own

I cannot strain my thoughts

But my actions, yes, my actions stir

An unrest in the pots.

I learn to still my painted wing

And flutter my decent hands.

My scrawl is messy and I know

I indeed know nothing of the lands

But waves of skin are all I see

I feel as though I'm lump

And I hate the fact that my words come out

Like they're just another bump.

72

In the end

After I have held

My vocabulary chart

To my heart

I'll know I'm me,

But what will happen

When I get lost

At sea?

73

You have lived one thousand lives

With a thousand tales, comes a thousand knives

All in the form of one thousand times

And with that, one thousand minds.

You will see one thousand things

And one thousand things will see you

One thousand eyes, one thousand hearts

But how many of them will be you?

74

I sense the gold

Of men not bold

And run away

From their casket mold

Then vary truth

Of boys named Ruth

And my coins are stolen

But the token

Erase my chest

And heart as best-

As I can

From the crooked fans

"I'll wait a while

For the call"

And load the boat

Then wait till fall.

75

Oh my little friend of time,

You think you are so kind.

We brush up on your

Literature

We brush up on your

Mind.

We see the scars you're holding,

Right along with paper-print.

The ants you see are scolding

You

For not giving us a hint.

76

Grassy eyes

And

Flower shoes.

Please-ignore

The pencil cues.

77

There are crickets in my clothes

And I don't know what to do

They itch and scream a bunch

And it isn't something new.

There are crickets in my clothes

Digging deep into my skin

Knowing that they can't be sated

By just the places I have been.

There are crickets in my clothes

Sewing strings into my arms

Looking closely at their leaders

That will soon control my charms.

There are crickets in my clothes

Pulling myself into straight lines

Making me sit and staple fingers

And so my actions aren't mine.

There are crickets in my clothes

Telling me what to say

Pushing past my lips to whisper

What I think of every day.

There are crickets in my clothes

And there is no where I can go

I cannot itch and scream a bunch

And so no one can ever know.

78

Red Red Red roses

Brought

Red

Red

Red blood.

(Down her fingers as the gift pressed into her hands.)

The lovely color enveloped her being

And it;

Consumed

Consumed

Consumed

Her.

79

I fell inside a pool of fish

Just how to start my day.

I'll get the tea,

The church is free,

And lug the manner away.

I've always hated company

So please go away.

Through your eyes you cannot see

"I'll come again later today."

You never made much sense to me.

I see you as a ghost.

But tea is nice,

There is no spice,

And the herb-lady makes a good host.

80

His shadow is a dragon

That climbs upon the bricks

Of a house where they stored children

In little tiny bits.

His last words are on a tombstone

That's made out of a ladder

And the rungs are filled with colors

That hallucinate small chatter.

A train that's filled with water

Will seep into his hometown

And the ghosts skate on their boards

Past the women with a frown.

And he can read the words

In the smoke outside the ferry

So he burns down the newspapers

That he finds in the library.

A tablecloth of snow

With rusting people to take flight

Sit on a creaking table

As the chairs start up a flight.

For in space there is a boat

That brings back all the stars

Who hang their colors in the meadows

Where the giants bring the cars.

When he claps, tornadoes

Stand up and start to dance

In a gala for the interest

With arthritis in their hands.

A house that holds the secret

With a bottomless abyss

Has eyes inside the wood

That's rather hard to miss.

He grew up with someone fake

Who never saw the molten

That forced the wings of angels

Onto the mantle for a token.

His childhood tries to melt away,

The circus starts to float

And someone takes off their face

And throws it in a moat.

In the ocean, there is space,

At least that's what he's told

But it's getting very

Late

And he's getting very

Old.

Who would swallow paint

Just to blow it all right out?

The exit sign is up ahead

Yet still the cactus pouts.

His shadow is a dragon

That morphs itself with wind

So he finds that broken cylinders

Are not the best place to begin.

81

And now the start, and now the end

Of things he'll never say,

And now the start, and now the end

Of things he did today.

And if he feels, for a moment only

Like what he did could help,

Then just how bad, let him ask

Could the ending have turned out?

82

Little one

My stories are simple

When printed in red

As you're sleeping so soundly

In a coffin-like bed

All waiting as daylight

Comes steers its own head

And finished as

I prepare

A feast when you're dead

83

I watch her, passing by

Someone I saw falling from the sky

Playing songs on violin

And I never asked her why

But she seemed like she was seeing

Feeling content with just being

And her song came from within

Her little tin-made violin

84

My shadow falls

Underneath walls

I can not

Lose my

Head.

For the cracks inside the ceiling

Do not make a comfy bed

Though

Placing strings on boards

To help with falling chords

And on the red-spiked piles, neatly filed,

We will find that we are dead

85

There are things that you must know

I tell you in great haste

My handwriting gives it away

Not just the things you've faced.

There's a monster that is coming

And he wants to keep your mind

I know you don't believe me

But you're running out of time.

There's a game you think you're playing

But it already wrote its end

Before you put down all your cards

And started to pretend.

There's a consequence to lying

And I know you do not care

But the moves that he is making

Have an outcome that's not fair,

There's a warning in my letter

I pray you take it quick

I will not be around to see

What really makes him tick.

There's a killer at your door

He was at mine before this sent

I can save you but what you must know

Is that you won't find where he went.

86

Help me to define a word

That no one's ever heard

A site, or situation,

In which no one is concerned.

87

They bound the ground

Of living breath

And never mind

The birds that rest

The man we take

Awaits his trial

His blood will spill

Over the tile

I walk right in

To cells that grate

The guards are sure

They need to wait

At last I meet

The man of two

Who's heads all spin

At someone new

A different kind of fear I see

From one with nothing to gain

But never has he seen someone

Stare down in such disdain

"I used to be a king." He spits

But never will that do

I answer with a side-step bow

"*Look how your kingdom treated you.*"

And answer with him will not take

For I have things to run

And the cell awaits another one

Whose trials have just begun

Then as I find the silver band

Tied strictly to my gun

I turn his heads straight into sand

And with my word, he's done.

88

Though all these songs

Fashioned in their own lovely crystal-gleam

Have been told to say the exact same thing

It

Saddens

Me

That they float on by

The molten, lovely, canvassed-sky.

89

I'd never say you are the worst

But you did in the past

And now, dare I, I think you're cursed

And how long will you last?

The cold of snow

Around me sees

And hidden foes

Around me freeze

And though you try your best to go

You fear it will stay still

And how am I, a child, to show

What lies over your hill?

For across land

Of shadowed breeze

My friends all play

With subject ease

The broken things you hide all say

That chagrin is to blame

But never have I seen you pray

About your coming fame.

You lay too still inside your bed

Then pen around your wrist.

I start to cry

As the ink dries

Forever in your fist.

90

I should not have a body

For it doesn't fit my mind

My legs do not work properly

And my fingers never rhyme.

My head is just too heavy

And my eyes are not my own

My stomach thinks his own thoughts

And though I do, I shouldn't grow.

I should not have a body

I do not belong in here

I think it very loudly

And I do not hold it dear.

So I'll cover up this body

Because I want no one to see

This flesh I am forced to live in

Because I swear it isn't me.

91

Pillows

Covered up my hideout

But do you really exist?

I'm getting very lonely

And my brain has turned to mist

And

There are some worthless moments

We can call them all by name

Yet we will not sit together

Because I know I'm very lame.

92

Is there perfection in this horror?

Rocking back and forth in sleep

Taking hold of all the sockets

That make thinking run way deep?

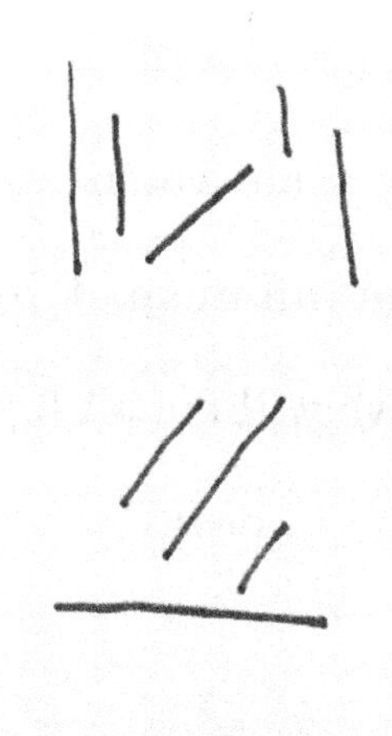

93

There are painted, gold-stone pathways

That the dead ones dance across

And a dying corpse will hate to lay

In a temple of grey moss

Then the core will shift and tilt

And turn the shower on-

Please. For a tub filled with glitter

Will stop catastrophe with ease

And a sticky residue

Left by guardians at most, are

Breaking molds created

By an ever-dreaming host

Who

Created many statues, then burned down all the books

And placed upon his bone-made shelf, a thing that never looks

And spoke to wandered children

In silent, aching screams

That

"*To climb your falling mountain*

You can't do as you please."

We don't know his extra stories

Or the template of his lines

Yet he shelves off all the fables that he has heard over time

And we don't know what he could do

If they all came to and held their knife

Because a picture tells a thousand words

So what about his life?

It doesn't fit, it never does

So what more can he do? When every bit of falling earth

Stays as far away from you

As

Possible. And waiting,

He picks up all the words

And glues them back together

And they fly away as birds.

94

There are doors beneath the floors

And floors that turn to doors

I am out of breath in mind

Am I running out of time?

These carvings I have made

Every one turns out the same

Is there reason in the signals

That have all become engrained-

In the doors that make the floors

And the floor we know as doors

Stopping madness from ensuing

In the cracks in the wall pursuing

All the things I am not inclined on doing

As my brain tells me to stop moving

All these things that last for hours

Searching gently for not-powers

Breaking all the little feelings

That have made my life worth meaning

Melting faces from these places

That I know are not disapproving

95

He was a wretched, cruel monster.

Long and spindly

With claws inside his teeth

And teeth inside his claws.

And they never thought he'd be protecting

Something oh so very small.

96

"I'm afraid you'll have to go on home,

I'm sorry I'm not there.

But humans seem to fear the things

Without a face and hair.

But through my watch I'll always be

Protecting you from here,

Another world away,

And I know I can't always be there.

But please stay still and do not fret

Of the monsters you have faced;

I know how to keep them away from you

When it's getting very late."

97

I never fear what comes on in

As night time rears its head,

For not all monsters that sneak by

Hide underneath my bed.

I never fear the monsters here

When the skies get really mad,

For I've found, that making sound

Doesn't make all monsters bad.

98

A little boy of three

Sat inside a shell of green

When an old lady of plenty

Decided her shell was empty

And passed it off again

To a girl of only ten

And the little boy decided

That her shell had been misguided.

99

Dead birds as leaves,

Across the trees-

Will dance of vines

And swing from eaves.

They're all-

(I swear)

Afraid of heights.

So they sing songs-

About their frights.

Such pretty voices that sing of fear!

They all pray that we all hear,

And help them down before they fall-

And fly across that golden hall.

And one day a bird will choose;

To kill the life he would wish to loose,

And all he saw was his demise-

When he looked through those big red eyes.

100

There is a band of mad men

Who wear yellow in the rain

And torment the lonely lookers

From chasing off their grain.

101

Someone was in my house

Ticking right along with time

They snuck right past the locks

And seeped straight into my mind

My dog told me he heard the knocking

But I knew there were no doors

That could hold a ghost from taking

Something that isn't yours

My hands then started rotting

Every lock was frozen shut

As this someone that was in me

Made her way down to my gut

My tongue then started falling

As she ate at every mouse

I never got to tell my family that

Someone was in my house.

102

Mallory

Then says

"*Erratic and Unnecessary*"

He has seen hereditary

Days

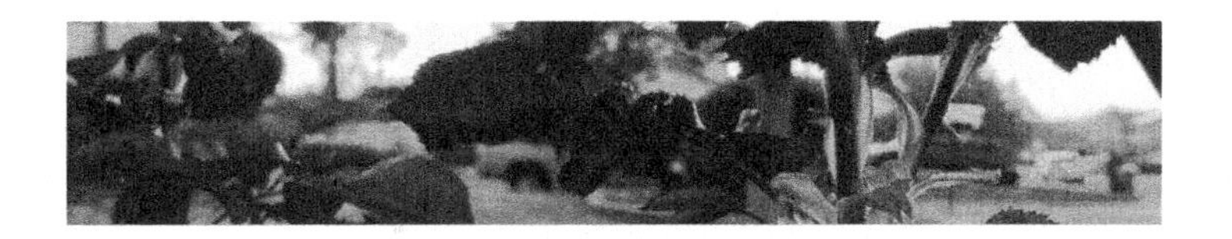

103

I wish I could tell you not to be afraid

And I'm so sorry that you

Cannot be okay

I am full of way too much

I don't knows

And that's just how my

Story goes.

Take a look at all my little friends

If it will help you

In the end

Comforting is not

My main trait

And there's nothing more

I hate

Than seeing this happen when

You cough

And watching your head fall off

104

Do you feel the grumbling?

Starting way below the earth

Like little giants stumbling

As their walking ways give birth

Have you figured out their motives?

In a place that has no 'when'

Sleeping in their dirt-made hallways

"*The wind is making noise again.*"

105

Taped together

In a mind

Of someone never finding kind

Then always being bubbly

His waiting for a list

He will tell you it is lovely

At the failing of a gift

To make this something nice.

A worthless being running high

"*I am afraid I am not good.*"

And many wonders make her cry

Inside the world that's made immortal

And they all make him want to die

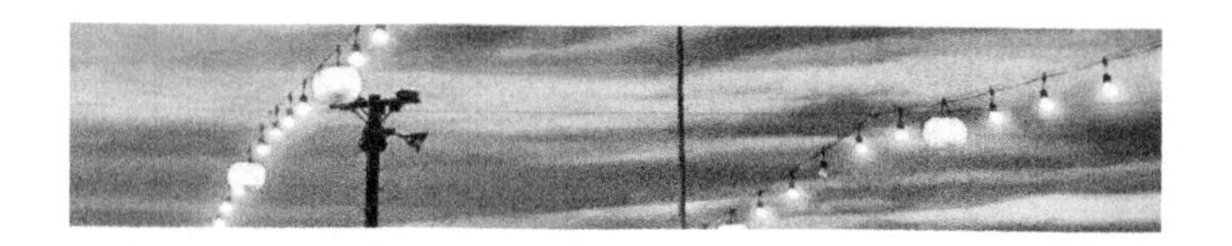

Erratic

and

Unnecessary

Made in the USA
Middletown, DE
25 January 2020